Wedding Toasts

Finding the Perfect Words

Jo Packham

Sterling Publishing Co, Inc., New York
A Sterling/Chapelle Book

Chapelle Ltd.

Owner: Jo Packham

Editor: Linda Orton

Images ©Copyright 1998
PhotoDisc, Inc.

Staff: Ann Bear, Areta Bingham,
Kass Burchett, Marilyn Goff,
Holly Hollingsworth, Will Jones,
Susan Jorgensen, Barbara Milburn,
Karmen Quinney, Leslie Ridenour,
Cindy Stoeckl, Gina Swapp,
Sara Toliver

Library of Congress Cataloging-in-Publication Data Available

10 9 8 7 6 5 4 3 2

A Sterling/Chapelle Book

Published by Sterling Publishing Company, Inc.
387 Park Avenue South, New York, NY 10016
© 2000 by Jo Packham
Distributed in Canada by Sterling Publishing
% Canadian Manda Group, One Atlantic Avenue, Suite 105
Toronto, Ontario, Canada M6K 3E7
Distributed in Great Britain and Europe by Cassell PLC
Wellington House, 125 Strand, London WC2R 0BB, England
Distributed in Australia by Capricorn Link (Australia) Pty Ltd.
P.O. Box 6651, Baulkham Hills, Business Centre, NSW 2153,
Australia

Sterling ISBN 0-8069-7387-0

Jo Packham is the founder and President of Chapelle, Limited, a Utah-based corporation. Chapelle's day-to-day operations are directed from offices located on Historic 25th Street in Ogden, Utah, nestled at the base of the Rocky Mountains. In the past 21 years, Chapelle has authored, packaged, or copublished over 400 titles on subjects ranging from wedding flowers to master woodworking, equaling over two million copies sold.

Chapelle is associated with the most respected designers, authors, and craftsmen—in all fields of arts and crafts—and has established an unquestionable reputation of quality and innovation. Chapelle titles are regularly featured as both main and alternates for every major book club around the world.

Jo has personally authored a series of twelve titles on wedding decoration and protocol, a publication on scrapbooking, *The Complete Book of Scarves*, and *Making Fabulous Pincushions*. She is married and the mother of two grown children.

Every effort has been made to ensure that all of the information in this book is accurate.

If you have any questions or comments, please contact:

Chapelle Ltd., Inc.
P.O. Box 9252
Ogden, UT 84409

Phone: (801) 621-2777
FAX: (801) 621-2788
e-mail: chapelle@chapelleltd.com
website: www.chapelleltd.com

Table
of
Contents

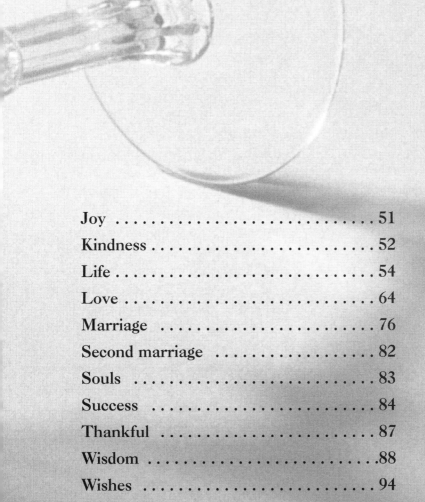

Introduction

A health to you,
A wealth to you,
And the best that life
 can give to you.
May fortune still be
 kind to you,
And happiness be
 true to you,
And life be long and
 good to you,
Is the toast of all your
 friends to you.

The custom of drinking a toast to the prosperity, happiness, luck, or good health of another dates back to antiquity. It is impossible to pinpoint the moment when the first crude vessel was raised in honor of an ancient god. What we do know is that the custom of drinking to health permeated the ancient world and that over time the simple act of toasting one another became embellished and intertwined with other customs. At some point along the way, toasts became a basic form of human expression and were created to convey deep feelings such as love, hope, high spirits, and admiration. They are used to celebrate success, happiness, and any or all other emotions or events worth honoring. A toast can be sentimental, emotional, cynical, lyrical, comical, defiant, long, short, or even just a single word.

Some time after the seventeenth century, the gesture of clinking glasses became popular. One legendary explanation for such glass clinking is that all five senses should come into play to get the greatest pleasure from a drink. It is tasted, touched, seen, smelled, and—with the clink—heard.

Etiquette of Wedding Toasts

Why make a wedding toast? Simply to express to the bride and groom—and to family members, friends, and other wedding participants—words of love, hope, and gratitude; to relay information; or simply because it is "tradition".

Traditionally, the first toast, usually given by the bride's father or an old family friend, is longer and ends with the wish of health and lasting happiness to the bride and groom. At the end of the toast, he raises his glass and toasts to the bride and groom, all guests raise their glass and join in the toast. The bride places her arm through the groom's and both drink. This locking of arms signifies the intertwining of new lives. The second toast is given by the bridegroom as a reply to the first and is concluded with specific words directed to the bridesmaids. The best man then replies on behalf of the bridesmaids, and will conclude his toast with words to the parents of the bride and groom.

The weddings of today, however, are much more flexible and toasts can be given in any sequence or manner that is chosen by the bride and groom. The

*Here's to the groom with
  bride so fair,
And here's to the bride
  with groom so rare!
Here's to the husband
  and here's to the
  wife;
May they remain lovers
  for life.*

important thing to remember—in relation to the giving of toasts—is to decide well in advance who will be toasting when, and, of course, to let them know so that they have ample time to prepare.

The Timing of Toasts

Circumstances and ideas for the when and where of giving toasts vary in different countries, with different religions, and according to different customs. However, if a basic guideline is needed, it could be as follows:

When toasts are presented at seated dinners for lengthy, formal wedding receptions, they begin after all eating at the formal meal has finished. If the meal is concluded with tea, coffee, drinks, and a wedding cake, speeches should be made after the cutting of the cake.

If the celebration is to continue throughout the evening and the wedding cake is to be served later, simply delay the cutting of the cake until after the toasts which conclude the formal meal.

If the wedding is very formal and a toastmaster is appointed, it is essential that he have a loud voice and extroverted personality. He may introduce the first and every subsequent person who wishes to give a toast, or he may only

To the bride and groom:

There are only two lasting bequests we can hope to give our children. One of these is roots, the other wings.

Hodding Carter

introduce the initial speaker. If no toast-master is included, the duties fall to the best man.

If the wedding is informal or a buffet, the toasts are offered at the beginning of the cake-cutting ceremony.

Preparing Your Toasts

When first sitting down to write your toasts, it is advisable to ask yourself why you have been asked to speak. Is it because you are closely related to the bride and groom or other members of the family; because you are old and wise and expected to give advice; or because you are an extrovert and known for your humor, wit, and "wisdom?" Whatever the reason, the toast should be prepared accordingly.

Remember: it is important to leave yourself enough time before the wedding to give sufficient consideration to what you would like to say. Do any necessary research, write your toast down and review it on several different occasions, and practice so you are familiar with the words that will convey so much to so many.

It is important to decide on the length of your toast before you begin researching and writing. Too short and it may seem unimportant, unplanned, or rude; too long and it may lose its intended meaning and bore the guests. Remember: your toast will reflect not only on those you are speaking to or about, but upon yourself.

Almost all of us need to conduct some form of research before speaking in front of a large gathering. Begin your research by looking for ideas, events, or thoughts on which you can elaborate. Talk with the parents, friends, relatives, or members of the wedding party. Talk with persons whose speaking abilities you admire. Find and read books on quotes and speeches.

When researching speeches, jokes, quotations, inspirational or religious words, poems, lines from songs or movies, or proverbs, remember you can use them directly and quote the author or you can adapt them to the person or the occasion.

When preparing your toast, keep in mind the following:

- After compiling your research, structure your notes in a logical interesting manner.
- List the essentials to be included and consider your opening remarks.
- Avoid stereotyped ideas if possible.

*Two such as you with
such a master speed
Cannot be parted nor be
swept away
From one another once
you are agreed
That life is only life
forevermore
Together wing to wing
and oar to oar.*
        *Robert Frost
        (1874–1963)*

- Delete anything that may be in questionable taste to any member of the festivities and if in doubt, leave it out.
- Avoid negatives, regrets, criticisms, hurtful jokes or comments, sexual innuendoes, and any sentiments that are vague or foolish.

Once your toast is completed and written down, read it aloud to yourself to be certain the sentences are not too long and you are not stumbling over them. Make certain the sequence of thoughts is logical, the wording is sincere, and the delivery is spontaneous. Change words or phrases that are redundant and eliminate any segment that may be considered controversial.

Let us celebrate this occasion with wine and sweet words.
Latin Proverb

Finally check your toast to make certain it complements the other toasts and speeches that are to be given by others. Be certain that you know the name of the previous speaker so that you can say, "Thank you, Michael," confident that his name is not Samuel!

The final step is the delivering of your toast. Perhaps the most important rule to follow when making your toast is to make certain that you are informed on your subject and that you speak with a most sincere heart.

Take three deep breaths before it is time for you to begin:

- Relax.
- Smile.
- Stand up straight, but stand comfortably.
- Keep your head up.
- Make eye contact with the person or persons you are addressing.
- Speak confidently, slowly, loudly, and with emotion, emphasis, and inflection.

A few suggestions for a most successful toast are:

1. Be brief. The person who has "a message to deliver" need only speak a few simple words of human interest to be assured they never lack an audience.

2. A toast on any occasion depends on whether the speaker has something to say, or whether you merely have to say something.

3. Avoid mixing toasts with other messages.

4. Be careful of a too flamboyant oratory style.

5. Avoid getting ahead of yourself.

6. Be careful not to talk above the heads of your audience.

7. Avoid admonishing, "lecturing", or giving too much instruction in your toast. Your audience expects to be entertained, not instructed.

8. Remember, you are the center of attention while toasting. Not only your words, but your appearance, expression, and attitude are on display. Remember, too, that you are a friend who was asked to share a very special moment and that one of the most popular toasts of all time was written for you alone: "Lord, fill my mouth with worthwhile stuff and nudge me when I've said enough!"

Seek a happy marriage with wholeness of heart, but do not expect to reach the promised land without going through some wilderness together.
Charlie W. Shedd

9. When proposing a toast, make certain you know what you are drinking.

Other "Wedding" Occasions for Traditional Toasting

The Engagement Party: After the guests have assembled, the father of the bride-to-be proposes a toast to his daughter. Her fiance answers with a

13

toast to his future bride and her family; other toasts follow.

Bachelor Party: The groom presents a toast to the bride and everyone raises his glass. Some go so far as to break the glass once the toast has been concluded, so that it may never be used for a less worthy cause.

Bachelorette Party: The bride proposes a toast to the groom and everyone raises her glass.

Rehearsal Dinner: First, is the customary salute to the couple by the best man. The groom follows with a toast to the bride and his new in-laws; then the bride toasts the groom and his family. Others may follow as they wish.

General Rules of Toasting

Guests should not enter or leave during the toasts, since it is distracting to the audience and disconcerting to the speakers.

When the festivities are over, members of the bridal party and guests will want to go up to the speakers and personally thank them for their toasts. In addition the bride and groom could express a thank you in the form of a short note.

To the bride from the groom:

Grow old with me!
The best is yet to be,
The last of life,
For which, the first
is made.
Robert Browning
(1812–1889)

Adversity

'Tis not so bad a world,
As some would like to make it;
But whether good or whether bad:
Depends on how you take it.

Where the willingness
is great, the difficulties
cannot be great.
>Niccolo Machiavelli
>(1469–1527)

What do you
live for, if it is
not to make life
less difficult for
each other?
>George Eliot
>(1888–1965)

When you get in a tight place and everything
goes against you, till it seems as if you could
not hold on a minute longer, never give up
then, for that's just the place and time the
tide will turn.
>Harriet Beecher Stowe
>(1811–1896)

Here's a toast to all who are here,
No matter where you're from;
May the best day you have seen
Be worse than your worst to come.

Those who never risk will never lose.
But neither will they grow.
Those who never feel will never cry.
But neither will they laugh.
Those who never love will never hurt.
But neither will they live.

One man in a thousand, Solomon says,
Will stick more close than a brother.
But the thousandth man will stand by
your side to the gallows–foot—after!
Rudyard Kipling
(1865–1936)

Advice

No man's advice is
entirely worthless.
Even a watch that
won't run is right
twice a day.

One of the great mysteries and dis-
coveries is that a human being can
alter his life by altering his attitude.

A guilty conscience is the
mother of invention.

Most of us only ask
for advice when we
know the answer but
want a different one.

Don't ever be afraid to admit you
were wrong. It is like saying you
are wiser today than you were
yesterday.

The worst sin towards
your (husband or wife)
is not to hate them, but
to be indifferent to them.
George Bernard Shaw
(1856–1950)

There is nothing so small
it cannot be blown out of
proportion.

You will notice that nothing you never
said will ever do you any harm.
Adapted from Calvin Coolidge
(1872–1933)

*I have noticed that nothing I never
said ever did me any harm.*
Calvin Coolidge
(1872–1933)

Why not today;
Mend a quarrel
Seek out a forgotten friend
Write a love letter
Share some treasure
Give a soft answer
Encourage youth
Keep a promise
Find the time
Forgive an enemy
Listen,
Apologize if you were wrong
Think first of someone else
Be kind and gentle
Laugh a little
Laugh a little more
Express your gratitude
Gladden the heart of a child
Take pleasure in the beauty
    and wonder of the earth
Speak your love
Speak it again
Speak it still once again.

Kathy Davis
The Time to be Happy is Now

Self-discipline is
when your con-
science tells you to
do something and
you don't talk back.

Take time to play—
It is the secret of perpetual youth.
Old English Prayer

I find the great thing
in this world is not so
much where we stand,
as in what direction
we are moving.
Oliver Wendell Holmes
(1809–1894)

We are continually faced with a series of
great opportunities brilliantly disguised
as insolvable problems.
John W. Gardner

Contentment is not the fulfillment of what you want,
But the realization of how much you already have.

Kiki Knickerbocker

Our greatest danger in
life is in permitting the
urgent things to crowd
out the important.

Oliver Wendell Holmes
(1809–1894)

Endurance is the crowning quality,
And patience all the passion of great hearts.

James Lowell Russell
(1819–1891)

There is nothing significant—nothing.

Samuel Taylor Coleridge
(1772–1834)

When you are right, you can
afford to keep your temper.
When you are wrong, you
can't afford not to.

He (she) that can have patience
can have what they will.
Adapted from Benjamin Franklin
(1706–1790)

*He that can have patience
can have what he will.*
Benjamin Franklin
(1706–1790)

Let go of the question
and the answer will
follow.

He who can suppress a
moment's anger may
prevent a day of sorrow.

He who permits himself to tell a
lie once, finds it much easier to
do it a second time.
Thomas Jefferson
(1743–1826)

All that a man gets by lying is that he is
not believed when he speaks the truth.

Experience is the
hardest kind of
teacher. It gives
you the test first,
and the lesson
afterward.
Unknown

The chains of habit
are generally too
small to be felt until
they are too strong
to be broken.
Samuel Johnson
(1709–1784)

You can observe a lot
by just watching.
Yogi Berra
(1925–1998)

Sometimes running
to grab the camera
forces you to miss
the photograph
entirely . . .

Each night pause and remember some
wonderful adventure, or lovely thing.

There is a pleasure in
the pathless woods.
Lord Byron
(1788–1824)

Consider how hard it is to change yourself
and you will understand what little chance
you have trying to change each other.

Criticism never built a house,
wrote a play,
composed a song,
painted a picture,
or improved a marriage.

Silence is one of the hardest
arguments to refute.

Silence is the ultimate
weapon of power.
Charles de Gaulle
(1890–1970)

Bachelor's Party

Drink, my buddies, drink with discerning,
Wedlock's a lane where there is no turning;
Never was owl more blind than lover;
Drink and be merry, lads; and think it over.

Comrades, pour the wine tonight
For the parting is with dawn;
Oh, the clink of cups together,
With the daylight coming on!
                    Richard Hovey

Here's to the lasses we've loved, my lad,
Here's to the lips we've pressed;
    For of kisses and lasses,
Like liquor in glasses,
    The last is always the best.

The four stages of man are infancy, childhood,
adolescence, and obsolescence.
        Art Linkletter *A Child's Garden of Misinformation*

Beauty

Have nothing in
your house that
you do not know
to be useful, or
believe to be
beautiful.
William Morris
(1834–1896)

Love wears a mask
at any age.
Unknown

Beauty is not in the face;
Beauty is a light in the heart.
Kahlil Gibran
(1883–1931)

Beginnings

Now this is not the end. It is
not even the beginning of the
end. But it is, perhaps, the end
of the beginning.
Winston Churchill
(1874–1965)

The past is but the beginning of a
beginning, and all that is and has
been is but the twilight of the dawn.
H. G. Wells
(1866–1946)

Celebration

Here's to you both—
a beautiful pair,
on the first celebration
of your love affair.

To your coming anniversaries—
may they be outnumbered only
by your coming pleasures.

The time to be happy
is now; the place to be
happy is here.
                Robert G. Ingersoll

To our host;
An excellent man;
For is not a man
Fairly judged by the
Company he keeps?

We've holidays and holy days, and memory days galore;
And when we've toasted every one, I offer one more.
So let us lift our glasses high, and drink a silent toast—
This day, deep buried in each heart, that we each love
the most.

Let us toast the health of the bride;
　　Let us toast the health of the groom,
Let us toast the person that tied;
　　Let us toast every guest in the room.

Down the hatch, to a striking match!

Here's to you and here's to me,
Wherever we may roam;
And here's to the health and happiness
Of the ones who are left at home.

　　Good day,
　　good health,
　　good cheer,
　　good night!

Celebrate the simple pleasures:
Awaken to nature's beauty
Rejoice in small miracles
Smile at a stranger
Hug the one you love
Be good to yourself
Build your bridge,
Sing your song,
Make your mark,
Don't forget to fly.
Stop waiting for tomorrow
The time to be happy is now

Kathy Davis
The Time to be Happy is Now

To the old, long life and treasure;
To the young, all health and pleasure;
To the fair, their face,
With eternal grace;
And the rest, to be loved at leisure.

Ben Jonson
(1572–1637)

'Tis hard to tell which is best,
Music, Food, Drink, or Rest.

> To the sun that warmed the vineyard,
> To the juice that turned to wine,
> To the host that cracked the bottle,
> And made it yours and mine.

Here's to your good health,
and your family's good health,
and may you all live long and prosper.
Rip Van Winkle

> Here's to us that are here, to you that are
> there, and the rest of us everywhere.
> Rudyard Kipling
> (1865–1936)

The most evident token and apparent
sign of true wisdom is a constant and
unconstrained rejoicing.
Michael de Montaigne
(1533–1592)

Communication

The most important aspect
of communication is to hear
what isn't being said!

A true diplomat is someone who
can tell you to go to hell in a way
that makes you look forward to
the trip.

Desires

A man travels the world over
in search of what he needs
and returns home to find it.
George Moore

Faith

For everyone who
asks receives; he
who seeks finds;
and to him who
knocks, the door will
be opened.

> Adapted from
> *Matthew 7:8*

*For everyone that asketh
receiveth; and he that
seeketh findeth; and to
him who knocketh, it
shall be opened.*

> *Matthew 7:8*

Sorrow looks back, worry
looks around, faith looks up.

Prayer changes everything.

I believe in mystery and miracles and the magic of a
   new day.
I believe in angels and natural wonder and the beauty
   inside of people.
I believe in rainbows and happy endings and dreams
   come true.
I believe in a bright-and-shining tomorrow ahead for
   me and you.

If you have faith . . . Nothing
will be impossible for you.
Adapted from *Matthew 17:20*

. . . If ye have faith as a grain
of mustard seed . . . nothing
shall be impossible unto you.
Matthew 17:20

Thank you for believing in me
before I believed in myself.
Kobi Yamada

If somebody believes in you,
and you believe in your dreams,
it can happen.
Tiffany Bangs

We never have more
than we can bear.
H. E. Manning

Faith consists in
believing when it
is beyond the
power of reason
to believe.
Voltaire
(1694–1778)

I have lived to
thank God
that all my
prayers have
not yet been
answered.

Come, Lord Jesus,
Be our Guest, and let
Thy gifts to us be blessed.
Amen.

All that I have seen
teaches me to trust
the Creator for all I
have not seen.
Ralph Waldo Emerson
(1803–1882)

If the only prayer you
say in your whole life
is "thank you," that
would suffice.
Meister Eckhart

God hath promised
Strength for the day,
Rest for the labor,
Light for the way . . .
Annie Johnson Flint

Some things have to be believed to be seen.
Ralph Hodgson

Forgiveness

Many promising reconciliation's have
broken down because, while both parties
came prepared to forgive, neither party
was prepared to be forgiven.

The weak can never forgive.
Forgiveness is the attribute of
the strong.

Mahatma Gandhi
(1869–1948)

When the heart is right, "for"
and "against" are forgotten.

Love understands and
therefore forgives.

Friendship

It was the excitement of making a new best friend—
the best, the purest feeling I have ever known.

Keith Hale

Thanks for being my go-everywhere-do-everything,
tell-each-other-anything, forget-our-troubles, like-the-
same-stuff, laugh-till-it-hurts, together-or-apart . . .
pick-up-where-we-left-off, be-ourselves, keep-each-
other's-secrets, have-fun-doing-whatever, couldn't-
want-a-better, always-and-forever friend.

You are always there when I need you . . .
a smile when I am down,
tissues when I cry,
praise when I do well,
advice when I ask,
support when I am unsure,
pride when I succeed,
and a friend when I am in need . . .

I'm as dear to you as he,
He's as dear to me as thee,
You're as dear to him as me,
Here's to "Three's good company."

How can it be, except by the miracle of
friendship, that someone can know you
so well even though you have told him
virtually nothing about your life?

Carlos Menot

As long as your conscience is your
friend, never mind about your enemies.

Conscience warns you as a friend
before it punishes you as a judge.

Some friendships are created by nature,
some by interest,
and some by souls.

Jeremy Taylor

It is around the table that friends
understand best the warmth of
being together.
Old Italian Saying

The world is gay and colorful,
And life itself is new.
And I am grateful for
The friend I found in you.

May the friends of your youth be
the companions of your old age.

Old friends are scarce,
New friends are few;
Here's hoping I've found
One of each in you.

Future

Always and forever;
Live, laugh, and love.

May you always be happy,
And live at your ease;
Get a kind husband
And do as you please.

J. S. Ogilvie
The Album Writer's Friend–1881

A life spent making mistakes
is more honorable but more
useful than a life spent doing
nothing.

George Bernard Shaw
(1856–1950)

There is a captivating quality about
people who devote themselves passion-
ately to creating a beauty, born of their
own vision, and who are willing to
wait to harvest their dreams.

Nancy Lindemeyer
Victoria Magazine–May 1990

What you do
speaks so loudly
that I cannot hear
what you say.

It is easier to suppress
the first desire than to
satisfy all that follow it.
Benjamin Franklin
(1706–1790)

Logic is a systematic way of coming to
the wrong conclusion with confidence.

Einstein's Three Rules . . .
1. Out of clutter find simplicity.
2. From discord make harmony.
3. In the middle of difficulty lies opportunity.

The best thing about the future is that
it comes only one day at a time.
Abraham Lincoln
(1809–1865)

Your interest should be in the future, because you
are going to spend the rest of your life there.
Adapted from Charles Kettering (1876–1947)

My interest is in the future, because I am
going to spend the rest of my life there.
Charles Kettering (1876–1947)

Gratitude

O Thou who has given us so
much, mercifully grant us one
thing more—a grateful heart.
George Herbert

Caring is everything.

Happiness

If you tickle yourself,
You can laugh when you like.
Chinese Proverb

Those who bring sunshine
to the lives of others cannot
keep it from themselves.
Sir James M. Barrie
(1860–1937)

May you be happy and
your enemies know it.

If you want to be happy,
    Begin where you are,
Don't wait for rapture
    That's future and far.
Begin to be joyous, begin to be glad
    And soon you'll forget
That you ever were sad.
Jo Petty

The true light
is that which
emanates
from within,
and reveals
the secrets of
the heart and
soul, making
it happy and
contented
with life.

Kahlil Gibran
(1883–1931)

To find happiness you must seek
for it in a focus outside yourself.

D. Beran Wolfe, M. D.

If you're determined
to be unhappy, you
probably will be.

Madeline L'Engle

You can't have
everything.
Where would
you put it?

Steven Wright

. . . he that is of a cheerful
heart hath a continual feast.

Proverbs 15:15

Happiness is as a butterfly, which,
when pursued, is always just beyond
your grasp, but which, if you will sit
down quietly, may light upon you.

Nathaniel Hawthorne

The really happy man
is the one who can
enjoy the scenery when
he has to take a detour.

Kathy Davis
The Time to be Happy is Now

Happiness resides
not in possessions
and not in gold;
the feeling of hap-
piness dwells in
the soul.

Democritus

Heart

A friend is someone who reaches for
your hand . . . and touches your heart.

With my whole heart,
I have sought you.
> Adapted from
> *Psalm 119:10*

With my whole heart,
have I sought you.
> *Psalm 119:10*

The most precious possession that
ever comes to a man in this world
is a woman's heart.
> Josiah Gilbert Holland

To win at affairs of the heart,
one must indeed participate.

If you act from the heart you
can't make a mistake.

Your hearts are full of treasure untold.

The song of the voice is sweet,
but the song of the heart is the
pure voice of heaven.
Kahlil Gibran
(1883–1931)

Trust in your heart.
Martha Young

For where your treasure is, there
will your heart be also.
Matthew 6:21

When you're with a friend,
your heart has come home.

Emily Farrer

Thanks to the human heart
by which we live,
Thanks to its tenderness, its
joys, and fears.

Henry Wadsworth Longfellow
(1807–1882)

'Twas not into my ear
you whispered, but into
my heart.

Judy Garland
(1922–1969)

To love is to admire with the heart;
and to admire is to love with the mind.

Théophile Gautier
(1811–1872)

Humor

The great question which I have never
been able to answer is, "What does a
woman want?"

> Sigmund Freud
> (1856–1934)

As you ramble on through life . . .
whatever be your goal; keep your
eyes upon the donut and not the hole!

> Dr. Murray Banks

Some think a wife must
think like a man, act like
a lady, look like a girl—
and work like a dog . . .

Show me a man
who doesn't make
mistakes and I'll
show you a man
who doesn't do
anything.

> Theodore Roosevelt
> (1858–1917)

Joy

Parents' Toast
It is written:
"When children find true love,
   parents find true joy."
Here's to your joy and ours,
   from this day forward.

Rich are they who treasure
simple joys.

Kathy Davis
The Time to Be Happy Is Now

If ever you are to enjoy
life, now is the time . . .
Today should always be
your most wonderful day.
Adapted from Thomas Dreier

If ever we are to enjoy life,
now is the time . . .
Today should always be our
most wonderful day.

Thomas Dreier

May your pleasures
be boundless while
you have time to
enjoy them.

He that thinks himself
the happiest . . . really
is so.

C. C. Colton
(1780–1832)

I wish you all the joy you can wish.
The Merchant of Venice, Act III

The harvest you give
thanks for now will be
of a different kind. It
will be the reaping of
the joys you feel when,
despite time often harried
and confusing, loved
ones are safely gathered
at your side.

Adapted from Tricia Foley
Victoria Magazine

*The harvest we give
thanks for now is of a
different kind. It is the
reaping of the joys we
feel when, despite time
often harried and con-
fusing, loved ones are
safely gathered at our
side.*

Tricia Foley
Victoria Magazine

Kindness

Be ye kind one to another.
Ephesians 4:32

Speak kind words and you
will hear kind echoes.

Always be kinder than necessary.
Sir James M. Barrie
(1860–1937)

There is a destiny that makes us brothers;
None goes his way alone:
All that we send into the lives of others
Comes back into our own.
Edwin Markham

Life

Celebrate everyday!

May the clouds in your life
form only a background
for sunsets and rainbows.

Drink wine, and live here blitheful while ye may;
The morrow's life too late is,—live today!

To the Bride
Love, be true to her; Life, be dear to her;
Health, stay close to her; Joy, draw near to her;
Fortune, find what you can do for her,
Search your treasure-house through and through for her,
Follow her footsteps the wide world over—
And keep her husband always her lover.

Anna Lewis

Look through your
wife's glasses and see
life through her eyes.

I could do without many
things with no hardship—
you are not one of them.
Ashleigh Brilliant

May we breakfast with Health,
dine with Friendship, crack a
bottle with Mirth, and sup with
the goddess Contentment.

Here is the toast of the moon and the stars,
To the life that soon will be ours.

May you live all the
days of your life.
Jonathan Swift
(1667–1745)

May your lives be as beautiful
as a summer day with just
enough clouds to make you
appreciate the sunshine.

May blessings be upon your house,
Your roof and hearth and walls;
May there be lights to welcome you
When evening's shadow falls—
The love that like a guiding star
Still signals when you roam;
A book, a friend—these be the things
That makes your house a home.
Myrtle Reed

May you live
as long as
you want to
and want to
as long as
you live.

Rich as he is, not even
the emperor can buy
back one single day.
Chinese Proverb

To me, every hour of the day and night
is an unspeakable, perfect Miracle.
Walt Whitman
(1819–1892)

If you think you're confused, think
of poor Columbus. He didn't know
where he was going when he started.
When he got there, he didn't know
where he was, and when he got back,
he didn't know where he had been—
and he did it all on borrowed money.
Today, he is a hero.

The past is history,
The future is mystery.
But today is a gift,
Which is why it is called the Present.

Life is ours to be spent,
not to be saved.
D. H. Lawrence
(1895–1892)

Imitate the sundial's ways
Count only the pleasant days.
German Proverb

To See a World in a Grain of Sand
And a Heaven in a Wild Flower,
Hold Infinity in the palm of your hand
And Eternity in an Hour.
William Blake
(1757–1827)

May God grant you many years
to live, for surely he must be
knowing the earth has angels all
too few and heaven's overflowing!
                    Irish Blessing

Life is eternal; and life is immortal . . .
                    Rossiter Worthington Raymond

Dreams are real while they last,
can we say more of life?
                    Havelock Ellis
                    (1859–1939)

Life is a continuous process of living and learning, longing and losing, with loving and laughing
filling the empty spaces in between . . .

There is more to life than
just increasing speed.
Mahatma Gandhi
(1869–1948)

Sincerity is to speak as we
think, to do as we pretend
and profess, to perform what
we promise, and really to be
what we would seem and
appear to be.
John Tillotson
(1630–1694)

With every rising sun
Think of your life as just begun . . .
Ella Wheeler Wilcox
(1850–1919)

Whatever life may bring—whatever God may send,
No matter whether clouds lift soon or late—
Take heart and wait!
Grace Noll Crowell

Life is more fun when
you don't keep score.

I drink to the days that are.
William Morris
(1834–1896)

Don't be so concerned about
making a living that you don't
take the time to make a life.

In life, you can never do a kind-
ness too soon because you never
know how soon it will be too late.
Ralph Waldo Emerson
(1803–1882)

Life is a play; 'tis not its length,
but its performance that counts.
Seneca
(4 B.C.–A.D. 65)

We think in generalities,
but we live in detail.
Alfred North Whitehead
(1861–1947)

Nothing in life is to be feared.
It is only to be understood.
Marie Curie
(1867–1934)

So come, and slowly we will walk through
green gardens and marvel at this strange
and sweet world.
Sylvia Plath

We are all preaching an unspoken
sermon with our lives.

Unitarian Minister

Our noble selves—
may we never be less.

May you have enough happiness to keep you sweet;
enough trials to keep you strong; enough sorrow to
keep you human; enough hope to keep you happy;
enough failure to keep you humble; enough success
to keep you eager; enough friends to give you
comfort; enough faith and courage in yourself to
banish depression; enough wealth to meet your
needs; and enough determination to make each
day a better day than yesterday.

Here's to Eternity—may we spend it in as
good of company as this night finds us.

Love

Since we shall love each other,
I shall be great!

Sensual pleasure passes and vanishes in the
twinkling of an eye, but the friendship between
us, the mutual confidence, the delights of the
heart, the enchantment of the soul, these things
do not perish and can never be destroyed. I
shall love you until I die.

Voltaire to Mme. Denis
(1694–1778)

Drink to me only with thine eyes,
And I will pledge with mine;
Or leave a kiss within the cup,
And I'll not look for wine.

Ben Jonson
(1572–1637)

Our love is the greatest gift
we can give to one another.

At first glance I loved you
with a thousand hearts.
Mihri Hatun Turkish
(17th Century)

Your love is comfort in sadness,
quietness in tumult, rest in
weariness, hope in despair.
Marion C. Garretty

Our love is like the misty rain that falls
softly—but floods the river.
African Proverb

Searching for the beauty, I saw morning!
Looking for joy, I found no end.
Searching for peace, I found the evening;
Learning to love, I gained a friend.

A toast to love
and laughter
and happily
ever after.

The course of true
love never did run
smooth.
William Shakespeare
(1564–1616)

May your joys be as bright as
the morning, and your sorrows
but shadows that fade in the
sunlight of love.

Here's to the husband—and here's to the wife;
May they remain lovers for life.

And things can never go badly wrong
If the heart be true and the love be strong.
George Macdonald

Love is patient,
    love is kind . . .
Love does not delight in
    evil but rejoices with
    the truth.
It always protects,
    always trusts,
    always hopes
    always perseveres.
            Adapted from
        I Corinthians 13:4, 6–7

Charity suffereth long, and
    is kind; charity envieth
    not; charity vaunteth not
    itself, is not puffed up,
Rejoiceth not in iniquity, but
    rejoiceth in the truth;
Beareth all things, believeth
    all things, hopeth all
    things, endureth all
    things.
            I Corinthians 13:4, 6–7

Love believes all things,
Hopes all things,
Endures all things.
        Adapted from
        I Corinthians 13:7

To love you is miracle
enough for me.

There is no fear in love; but perfect love casteth out fear: . . .

I John 4:18

There is no surprise more magical
than the surprise of being loved.

Charles Morgan

Love is everything it's cracked up to be. That is
why people are so cynical about it . . . It really
is worth fighting for, being brave for, risking
everything for. And the trouble is, if you don't
risk anything, you risk even more.

Erica Jong

Real isn't how you are made . . . it is a thing
that happens to you when someone really
loves you. Then you become real.

The Velveteen Rabbit

Love is a place and through this
place of love move all places.

e. e. cummings
(1894–1966)

We can do not great things;
only small things with great love.

Mother Theresa
(1910–1997)

For one human being to love another . . . that
is perhaps the most difficult of all of our tasks,
the final and ultimate proof, the task for which
all others are but preparation.

R. Maria Rilke
(1875–1926)

A wondrous subtle thing is love.
Sir Arthur Conan Doyle
(1859–1930)

There is a silence, born of love,
which expresses everything.
Count Vittorio Alfieri

There is nothing holier in this life of ours
than the first consciousness of love—the first
fluttering of its silken wings—the first rising
sound and breath of that wind which is so
soon to sweep through the soul.
Henry Wadsworth Longfellow
(1807–1882)

The power to love is God's greatest
gift to man, for it never will be taken
from the blessed one who loves.
Kahlil Gibran
(1883–1931)

How do I say "Thank You"
to the angels above
Who've blessed our life
With their magical love?
Barbara Milburn

Love has nothing to do with
what you are expecting to
get—only with what you are
expecting to give—which is
everything.
Katherine Hepburn

Every house where love abides
and friendship is a guest,
Is surely home, and home sweet home
For there the heart can rest.
Henry Van Dyke

Love is what you've been
through with somebody.
James Thurber

It is when you get older and the tables
turn a little that you realize that getting
and giving love come as a package—that
finding someone to love is as important
as finding someone to love you.

There are many kinds of love, as many kinds of light;
And every kind of love makes a glory in the night.
There is love that stirs the hearts, and love that gives
    it rest,
But the love that leads life upwards is the noblest and
    the best.
                                        Henry Van Dyke

Love is only for the
young, the middle-
aged, and the old.

Love comforteth like
sunshine after rain.
William Shakespeare
(1564–1616)

Consider not the gift of the lover,
but the love of the giver.
Ellye Howell
*Dame Curtsey's Book of Novel
Entertainment for Every Day in the Year*

Cupid
His wing is the fan of a lady.
His foot is an invisible thing;
And his arrow is tipped with a jewel,
And shot from a silver string.
Verse from a nineteenth-century calling card

Remember always:
Love has no endings,
only beginnings.

Shouldn't the definition
of marriage be Love!?

Love from a Friend:
Long sought,
rarely found,
and forever kept.
True Friends

To love a person is to learn
the song that is in their
heart, and to sing it to them
when they have forgotten.
Thomas Chandler

People who love us for what
we are, not for what we have
done, are precious support
when we're trying to do and
be more.

Peter McWilliams

Trouble is a part of life, and if you
don't share it, you don't give the
person who loves you a chance
to love you enough.

Dinah Shore

I love you, not only for what you are,
but for what I am when I am with you.
I love you, not only for what you have
made of yourself, but for what you are
making of me.

Ray Crats

Marriage

Here's to my mother-in-law's daughter,
 Here's to her father-in-law's son;
And here's to the vows we've just taken,
 And the life we've just begun.

Only two things are necessary to keep one's
wife happy. One is to let her think she is having
her own way, and the other, to let her have it.
                                    Lyndon Johnson
                                     (1908–1973)

It is impossible for a woman to be married to the
same man for fifty years. After the first twenty-five,
he is not the same man.

To the Bride from the Groom:
When I take you in my life,
I now have four arms instead of two.
Two heads. Four legs.
Two possibilities for joy.
Sure, two possibilities for tears,
but I can be there for you while you cry
and you can be there while I cry,
because nobody should ever cry alone.

Marriage is a lot like the army,
everyone complains, but you'd
be surprised at the large number
that reenlist.

James Garner

Marriage is your faith in all that is good in
the world. Marriage is the selfless spirit of
doing for each other. Marriage is laughter
and friendship and the spreading of cheer,
and it is the guileless wonder of childlike
love. Marriage is the sweet joy of families
united, it is the tender knowledge that you
are loved by someone and that you have
someone to love. Marriage is believing in
prayer and the power that answers.

Here's to marriage, that happy estate that
resembles a pair of scissors: "So joined that
they cannot be separated; often moving in
opposite directions; yet punishing anyone
who comes between them.

Rev. Sydney Smith
(1771–1845)

Alone you can do so little,
together you can do so much.
Adapted from Helen Keller
(1880–1968)

Alone we can do so little,
together we can do so much.
Helen Keller
(1880–1968)

Marriage is a journey towards an unknown destination: The discovery that people must share not only what they don't know about each other, but what they don't know about themselves.

Marriage teaches you such important virtues as commitment, loyalty, dedication, perseverance, meekness, and many other things you wouldn't need if you had stayed single.

When the "honeymoon" is over and the day-to-day of marriage begins, always remember to be thankful for:

1. The alarm that goes off early in the morning because it means that you are alive.

2. The piles of laundry and ironing because it means your loved ones are nearby.

3. Your huge heating bill because it means that you are warm.

4. Lawns that need mowing, windows that need cleaning, and gutters that need fixing because it means you have a home.

5. The shadow who watches you work because it means you are out in the sunshine.

6. The mess to clean up after a party because it means you have been surrounded by friends.

7. The clothes that fit a little too snug because it means you have enough to eat.

8. The spot you find at the far end of the parking lot because it means you are capable of walking.

9. All the complaining you hear about your government because it means you have free speech.

10. The taxes you pay because it means you are employed.

11. The lady behind you in church who sings off-key because it means you can hear.

12. Weariness and aching muscles at the end of the day because it means that you have been productive.

Marriage is a rush into the unknown—
you can duck down and hope nothing
hits you or stand up as tall as you can
and look it straight in the eye . . .

Eventually, it's the silences which
made the real conversations between
friends (husband and wife). Not the
saying, but the never needing to say.
Margaret Lee Runback

Marriage is tough sometimes. There are a zillion
decisions to make and none of them is easy. There
are things you will want to do but can't, and
things you don't want to do but have to. There are
good times and hard times, and days you feel like
nobody could ever possibly understand what it is
like to be you—and you are probably right—but
your (wife/husband) is here to talk or forget about
life for just a little while. That's why you married
him/her. Don't ever forget . . .

The spirit within you remains a
free thing filled with countless
dreams to share.

Flavia Weeden

May you share all the days of your
marriage and may they be filled
with good friends, a forgiving family,
and contentment.

"Driven for mere existence is
not good enough," a chauffeur
to the soul once said.

I need so much the quiet of your love
After the day's loud strife.

Charles Hanson Towne

Second Marriage

The difficulties of life are
intended to make us better,
not bitter.

If marriage is to be a success,
one should begin by marrying
the right person.
                          Hermann Keyserling

A Second Marriage: To the triumph
of hope over experience.
                          Samuel Johnson
                          (1709–1784)

Souls

Take time to Laugh—
It is the music of the Soul
Old English Prayer

The temple of your purest
thoughts is silence.
Sarah J. Hale

Whatever souls are made of—
yours and mine are the same.
Emily Bronte
(1818–1848)

A soul friend is someone with whom I can share my
greatest joys and deepest fears, confess my worst
sins and most persistent faults, clarify my highest
hopes and perhaps most unarticulated dreams.
Adapted from Edward C. Sellner

*A soul friend is someone with whom we can share our
greatest joys and deepest fears, confess our worst sins
and most persistent faults, clarify our highest hopes
and perhaps most unarticulated dreams.*
Edward C. Sellner

Success

From the Bride:
All it took to get here was a
lucky star, a handful of dreams,
and a lot of hard work!

A good wife and health
Are a man's best wealth.

We is terrific.
Diana Ross

We are so much less without each other.
Leo Buscaglia

Nobility of character manifests itself
at loop-holes when it is not provided
with large doors.
Mary E. Wilkins Freeman

What one cannot, the other can.
William Deverant

The secret of success is
constancy of purpose.
Benjamin Disraeli
(1804–1881)

Coming together is a beginning;
keeping together is progress;
working together is success.
Henry Ford
(1863–1947)

To understand the heart and mind
of a person, look not at what he
has already achieved, but at what
he aspires to do.
Kahlil Gibran
(1883–1931)

He who has begun has
the work half done.
Horace
(65–8 B.C.)

Success is a journey,
not a destination.

Listen quietly, opportunity's
knocks are often very soft.

Let us toast the fools; but for them
the rest of us could not succeed.
Mark Twain
(1835–1910)

The Ten Commandments contain 297 words. The Bill
of Rights is stated in 463 words. Lincoln's Gettyburg
Address contains 266 words. A recent Federal direc-
tive to regulate the price of cabbage contains 26,911
words. When you have something important to say—
say it briefly.

Thankful

May you be thankful for
all the days of your life.

Here's to the blessings of the year,
Here's to the friends we hold so dear,
To peace on earth, both far and near.

To have someone who brings out the
colors of life and whose very presence
offers tranquility and contentment
enriches my being and makes me
grateful for the opportunity to share.
Kathleen Tierney Crilly

Wisdom

Woman is a miracle of
divine contradictions.
Jules Michelet
(1798–1874)

The greatest of all arts is
the art of living together.
William Lyon Phelps

Few things are quite
so embarrassing as
watching your spouse
do something you just
said couldn't be done.

A man who has committed a mistake
and doesn't correct it is committing
another mistake.
Confucius
(551–479 B.C.)

If you enjoy good health,
you are rich.

May you have the hindsight to
know where you've been . . .
The foresight to know where
you're going.

Charles M. Meyers

You shall and you shan't
You will and you won't
You're condemned if you do,
And you are damned if you don't!

One of the most serious thoughts
that life provokes is the reflection
that we can never tell, at the time,
whether a word, a look, a touch,
or an occurrence of any kind, is
trivial or important.

A bird does not
sing because it
has an answer,
it sings because
it has a song.

The only time a woman changes
a man is when he's a baby.
Natalie Wood
(1938–1981)

Does time ever stop for a
moment to catch us?

If someone puts a hot fudge sundae in
front of you, don't wait until it melts
before you eat it.

God wove a web of loveliness,
Of clouds and stars and birds,
But made not anything at all
so beautiful as words.
Anne Hempstead Branch

Always be yourself, after all,
who else is more qualified.

Our senses
Our instincts
Our imagination
Are always a step ahead
of our Reason
Octavio Paz

It is better to be silent
and be considered a
fool than to speak
and remove all doubt.

I hear and I forget, I see and I
remember, I do and I understand.
Chinese Proverb

Wise men learn from others'
mistakes, fools by their own.

A wise man sees as much as he
ought, not as much as he can.
Michael de Montaigne
(1533–1592)

Conscience: An inner voice that
warns us that somebody is looking.
H. L. Mencken
(1880–1956)

Much wisdom can be crowded into four words:
In God we trust.
This, too, shall pass.
Live and let live.
Still waters run deep.
Bad news travels fast.
Nothing succeeds like success.
Charity begins at home.
Nothing ventured, nothing gained.
Man proposes, God disposes.
Let sleeping dogs lie.

Wishes

May you live as long as you
Wish, and have all you Wish
as long as you live. This is
my wedding Wish for you.

Here's wishing you more happiness
Than all my words can tell,
Not just alone for your wedding day
But for all our years as well.

A wedding wish—
May you never forget
what is worth remembering
or remember what is best forgotten.

May the most you wish
for be the least you get.

And here's to ourselves
And wishing all
The wish they wish themselves!

Wishing you heaven in your
heart, starlight in your soul,
and angels in your life . . .

I wish you health; I wish you
wealth; I wish you gold in store;
I wish you heaven when you die;
what could I wish you more?

Index